Inside Cover Fig. **The Princess Elizabeth,** *aged about 13 c 1546*
Sometimes attributed to William Scrots
The Royal Collection at Windsor ©Her Majesty the Queen
Obtained from Google Images

Copyright © 2011 by Janette Elizabeth Lassiter-Smith. 103687-SMIT

ISBN: Softcover   978-1-4653-6816-4

The Elizabethan Era Gardener's Handbook: a scholarly reference and
how-to guide for a specific period style garden introducing verifiable
natural sixteenth century gardening information and techniques.

To order additional copies of this book, contact:
Xlibris Corporation
1-888-795-4274
www.Xlibris.com
Orders@Xlibris.com

Elizabethan Era Gardener's Handbook

Period Style Gardening

Janette Elizabeth Lassiter-Smith

Contents

Historical Background

Kenilworth Castle garden was originally situated in the town of Kenilworth in Warwickshire within the Midlands of Britain. The garden was surrounded by a lake that gave it the appearance of an island stronghold. Historians, archaeologists, gardeners, and other scholars (Elisabeth Woodhouse and Trea Martyn) have attempted to uncover the precise forms and structure[1] of this garden with varying levels of success. This overview of Elizabethan gardening utilizes a specific, surviving garden as a lens and recent discoveries about the history of the site, arranged in approximately chronological order, to illustrate the development of the site.

Conflicting historical accounts have assigned different dates to the origin of Kenilworth castle, but all agree that the garden experienced turbulent times, including changes of hand, constant construction, and re-construction. Each event had some significant bearing on its appearance. According to **Gardens of Warwick,** the siege warfare and violent insurrections that the garden experienced led to a series of historical distortions, renovations, and modifications.[9-13] Shifting ideological forces also brought great changes as different personalities sought to make the garden in their ideological image.

The earliest recorded reference to Kenilworth was in the year 1086 in the **Domesday Book.** The book describes the site as a small settlement of villagers in a forest clearing referred to as Arden and owned by the royal manor of Stoneleigh.[Woodhouse 111] It is 95 miles northwest from London and about five miles from Coventry, and a similar distance from Warwick. Its title and origin are attributed to a Saxon king of Mercia, of the name Kenulph and his son Kenelm. The suffix "worth" is from the Saxon, signifying a mansion or dwelling place. An up-to-date summary of the history of the area can be found in a web site **Kenilworth Castle,** managed by Anthony Corbett. [Corbett]

According to the above website, the castle existed during the reign of King Arthur. Early records describe the castle as having stood on a hill known as Hom during Saxon times. The castle was destroyed in a major battle that that pitted King Edmund against Canute II, then King of Denmark. It was not until a century later that the castle was rebuilt. The ownership of the castle was transferred by King Henry I to Geoffrey de Clinton, a Norman who served as the King's chamberlain. Being the emperor's treasurer and chief justice, Clinton established the castle in line with the expectations of his office. It has often been suggested that the original design of the castle was of motte-and-bailey type. A motte-and-bailey is a form of castle with a wooden or stone keep - a strong central tower - situated on a raised earthwork called a motte. There is also an enclosed courtyard, or bailey, surrounded by a protective ditch and palisade, a fence used as a defensive structure. There still remain physical forms at the site, including a ditch section, that give substance to this presumption. Clinton also commissioned the abbey of St. Mary on the site. He also built the structure known as Caesar's Tower, believed to have been erected between the years 1170 and 1180.[Corbett]

At the death of Clinton, the castle became crown property. The castle was caught up in the thirteenth century Baron's War, when forces under the charge of Henry III laid siege to the castle and Simon de Montfort, then Earl of Leicester, fiercely defended it. In the fourteenth century, John of Gaunt remodeled the building and attempted to provide an aesthetic change. Henry V, during his reign, created a lakeside banqueting house, and the modifications were increased at the time of Henry VIII, who put up new lodging facilities on the castle grounds.[Corbett]

According to *Gardens of Warwick*, the lands and titles were restored to Queen Elizabeth after a brief ownership by John Dudley, the father of Robert Dudley, in 1553.[5] Following John Dudley's execution, Elizabeth gave it to Robert Dudley, Earl of Leicester, in 1563. The various artistic representations in the garden design were meant to express ideologies similar to those represented in major works of literature popular during the Elizabethan epoch. Poets and writers of the Renaissance, such as Francis Bacon and Phillip Sidney,[2] nephew of Robert Dudley, were obsessed with the desire to articulate new aesthetic meanings that were radically different from the forms celebrated in works of ancient and medieval art. Moreover, this golden era abounded with men of genius, whose range of interests included art, science, and economy. The art of gardening profited handsomely during this time.

Fig. 1 Kenilworth Castle c. 1575. Obtained from media storehouse
id 1634417 www.mediastorehouse.com

Robert Dudley's conception of beauty as represented in the garden might be thought of as one bold effort to situate his ideological values such as strength, the natural world, and classical mythology into the garden. His effort, however, can never really be placed into a narrow ideological form, as his works also carry heavy forms of Greco-Roman art, which carried a wider range of meanings. Artistically, therefore, Dudley's imagination created a garden that might be thought of as an attempt to negotiate a merger between times, spaces, and different ideologies of his time and the past. The floral set-up, the aviaries, and the plantations appear to celebrate realism and simplicity. The sculptures, on the one hand, reflect antiquity while, on the other, they transposed the sceneries of the garden into a fantastic and mystical realm.[3]

The representation of the Kenilworth garden was meant to evoke very high romance; therefore, romantic signifiers were extensively used in art forms throughout the landscape. Dudley was at pains to capture the trappings of power that would represent his longings, above all else his romantic interest in the queen. Dudley's use of heraldic symbols - such as bears and a ragged staff - showcased his own pedigree, and the insularity of the garden showed the extent of Dudley's aspirations, making Kenilworth Castle garden strictly controlled and shielded from public view.[Dix 163] While this might be expected in the aristocratic tradition, the symbolic meaning of the private garden was that the whole project was aimed at isolating the garden visitor, literally and figuratively, from the ordinary discourse of life, securing the residence for royalty, even if only by association.[4]

Unfortunately, the site shared the disastrous hardships of its royal owners. Oliver Cromwell gave the whole property to officers of his army, who demolished many parts of the castle and sold many valuable materials. They also drained the great pool, cut down the woods, destroyed the parks and the chase, and divided the land among themselves. It was then given to Sir Edward Hyde by Charles II after the Restoration. Later, a series of titleholders held the property, and the titles of Baron Kenilworth and Earl of Clarendon were created for the estate.[Corbett] Then, through the eldest surviving daughter of the last earl of that family, it descended to the Earl of Clarendon, finally ending the devastation started by Cromwell.[Corrie] After some time, Kenilworth Castle was passed into the possession of John Davenport Siddeley, 1st Baron of Kenilworth. In 1958, his son gave it to the people of Kenilworth, and in 1984, English Heritage took over the role of maintaining the Castle.[Gardens in Warwickshire 12]

The sources regarding this site suggest that it is continually and rapidly changing. Although these changes are of great interest, at the same time, they create an intimidating historical problem, especially with regard to the site and to the landscape of its gardens. While records and illustrations survive in various forms, the grounds are no longer in original condition. Further, a garden can never be recreated as it was, even if that is the desire of the researcher, since nature constantly changes. If this most magnificent landmark can now be left to the slow advances of time, it is likely to remain a monument of once noble grandeur which many future ages may ponder.

Design and Structure

Kenilworth garden is an example of the Elizabethan style, which was usually regarded as eclectic. The influences that guided this art originated from an era of exploration, a time when overseas travelers brought back exotic plants and new forms of artwork. One fundamental feature was the creation of geometric hedge designs alongside statues and flowers. The immense beauty of the Kenilworth garden lies in its representation of Elizabethan aesthetics.

The design and structure of the Kenilworth Castle garden reflects the external forces that influenced its creation. The sixteenth century was a period defined by high geopolitical activities within and without the British Empire.[5] Transition was taking place in this region and across the continent as leaders sought change from the medieval model in an attempt to create a new ideal unique to the Renaissance. Locally, Britain sought to consolidate her power and progress among peers. Through solidarity and exploration, Britain would strengthen her position as a world power. Renowned men were engaged in the business of spreading her trade and relevance across Europe and breaking new ground in distant territories. Culture reflected what was happening on the political and imperial scene.[6]

England's earlier isolation meant that, until Kenilworth, gardens were based on French and Dutch designs. These, in turn, were mostly derived from Italian replicas, so they were translations of translations. Dudley introduced new ideas, such as the Greco-Roman terrace, into garden design. (Martyn 101) On the cultural front, patriotic artists blended the ideologies of cultural purity and the superiority of the British system in the forms of creative art, poetry, and music as well as gardens. When a visitor entered the grounds, a story unfolded that rivaled other gardens of the time. The British celebrated the qualities of their culture and couched them in ways that sought to place them above other systems. There was also a need to create treaties with willing neighbors, and this called for cultural exchanges with newly formed friends. Another concern was the spreading of British frontiers through empire. All forms of aesthetics were brought together to create an imaginative universe in which British culture was the central axis. The British subordinated or blended their indigenous art forms with foreign cultures and past civilizations.

These are only some of the forces that framed and directed Dudley as he went about recreating the Kenilworth Castle garden. The design and shape of the garden captured a form of universalism where Britain and her royal qualities were the center of the world's culture. The pomposity and creative extravagance of the garden together and separately served to illustrate this reality. Outdoor landscaping was constructed to align with the mix of traditional British aesthetics and borrowed artistic experiences. The Renaissance returned to value of the material world, a shift that can be seen in art forms showing the corporeality of the human body, and the three dimensional reality of landscape.

The outdoor patterning of the Kenilworth garden was made in a manner that reified its regal quality to align with the wishes and purpose of the garden, thereby making it more real as imagined by its creator. Gardeners and floral professionals have argued that there was an overwhelming sense of artistic extravagance in the substance and structure of the garden. [National Garden Clubs, Inc. 86] It is with consternation that one important group, **The National Garden Clubs, Incorporated,** does not reflect any information on period style gardening from the fifteenth or sixteenth century in their very important judging instructional manual. One sixteenth century painting of the garden survives. **Queen Elizabeth at Kenilworth,** dated 1575, by Marcus Gheeraerts the Elder shows a large garden by a lake with pleasure boats, including a gondola (see image below). At the far end of the garden, steep steps lead to a banqueting house. Elizabeth is shown walking along a terrace with Dudley and Sidney. However, the image may not record any actual garden and may be based on Continental engravings. [Martyn 104, 105]

Fig 2. Queen Elizabeth at Kenilworth c 1575 by Marcus Gheeraerts, the Elder.
Obtained from Google Images.

Flowers at Kenilworth Castle Garden

The Kenilworth Castle garden was decorated with scented flowers that represented Elizabethan qualities. The most commonly used were gilly flowers,[7] whose perfume could be smelled by visitors as they toured the garden. The choice of flowers was usually symbolic, deliberately chosen to accord with royal values and illustrating the life of Queen Elizabeth. One special feature about the roses[8] that grew in the garden was that they were made to peak around July, a time when Queen Elizabeth usually visited the garden. Other plants in the garden included cherries and apples. The variety was almost exclusively of traditional English taste, although some areas of the garden reflected aspects of French aesthetic culture.

The plants at the Kenilworth garden were arranged according to their uses. The geometrical shape of the garden would be arranged so that one side of the garden was decorated by edible flowers, while the other side would be lined with lawns of inedible flowers. This technique was repeated with the trees, so that the fruit trees and the non-fruit trees would be lined separately around the garden. The artistic intention was to create an ambience like that of the Garden of Eden.[9] The Elizabethan aesthetic tradition borrowed heavily from biblical allusions to the creation as a parallel to physical forms of art. Laneham relates his findings: "Let me tell you a little of the dignity of One-hood; wherein always all high Deity, all Sovereignty, Preeminence, Principality, and Concord, without possibility of disagreement is contained: As, One God, One Saviour, One Faith, One Prince, One Sun, One Phoenix; and One of great wisdom saith, One heart, One way". (Laneham 33) The royal life has always been regarded as a bastion of Christianity. Dudley must have intended to situate the aesthetics within the larger framework of Christian values, as represented and celebrated in the life of Queen Elizabeth I.

The floral allure at the garden was occasionally utilitarian but mainly served aesthetic aims. The use of mazes and labyrinths guided visitors to different sections of the gardens, and more specifically, they acted as physical indicators to the location of major artworks in the gardens. The shaping of the gardens was done in definite geometrical forms such as squares, triangles, circles, or rectangles. This arrangement could sometimes be used to separate the different kinds of flowers according to their purposes.

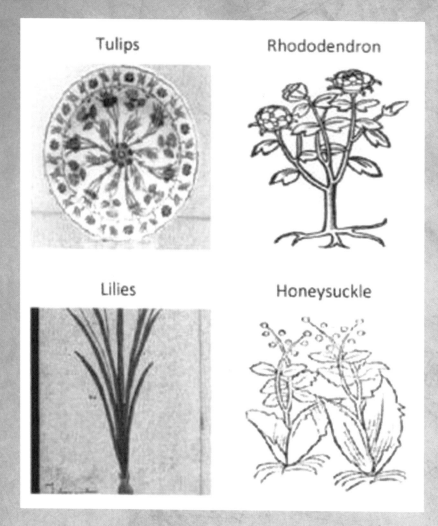

Fig. 3 Blooming Flora. Tulips[10], Rhododendron[11]. Lilies[12], and Honeysuckle[13].
Retrieved from ARTstor, Manuscripts and Early Printed Books.
The medieval ceramic decorative art and printed images can be found
at the Bodleian Library at the University of Oxford. England.

Some of the flowers featured prominently in the garden included blossoming flora such as tulips *(Tulipa sp.)*, ornamental bulbs with origins from Southern Europe and the Near East; rhododendron *(Nerium oleander)*,[14] a poisonous shrub from the Mediterranean; lilies[(English Heritage)] *(Lilium sp.)*, ornamental flowers, of which at least fifteen European and Near Eastern species were in cultivation; and honeysuckle *(Lonicera periclymenum)*, also called woodbine, a climbing shrub, natively grown for decoration and whose berries were occasionally used in medicine. In other sections of the garden, annuals could be planted. The most commonly used annuals included marigolds *(Calendula officinalis)*, ornamental and medicinal flowers from the Mediterranean, introduced about 1580, and pansies *(Heartsease sp.)*.[(Hill 10-17)]

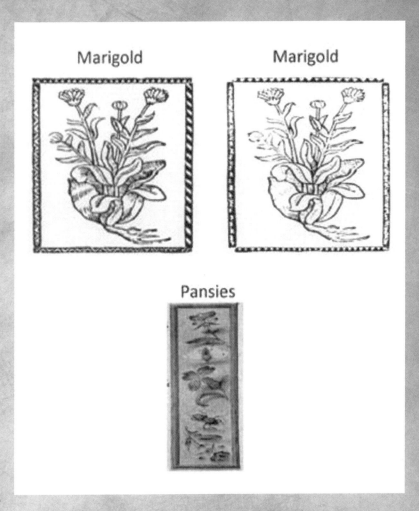

Fig. 4 Marigolds and Pansies. Retrieved from ARTstor, Manuscripts and Early Printed Books. Medieval images from "The Illustrated Bartsch," Vol. 90, show two sixteenth-century similar but not identical woodcuts. Historians reason that the inclusion of both these images in the same volume may never be discovered! Pansies obtained from "Book of Hours For the Use of Rome," in Latin, Illuminated Manuscript on Vellum.

However, roses have remained some of the most commonly used flowers in almost all forms of Elizabethan gardens. At least forty varieties of roses were in cultivation during sixteenth-century England. These included the multi-petalled Dutch or cabbage rose and the first musks and damasks, introduced from Asia.[Hill 15] Where some beautiful backdrops of flowers were desired, the gardeners could use trailing, bush forms, or climbing roses. The arbors were thought to have been covered with the eglantine rose, a symbol of virginity and a reference to Queen Elizabeth. The rose can be seen as a link between the spheres and wisdom. At this time, the concept that the queen's passions were controlled by her wisdom was advanced. The celestial sphere echoes this theme; it symbolizes wisdom and the queen's royal command over nature. The symbolism could easily have been "read" by Elizabeth and was multilayered with ambiguous intricacy - biblical, mythological and chivalric. (Mawrey and Groves 14,15)

Herbs and Vegetables at Kenilworth Castle Garden

In the Elizabethan context, herb gardens could be used between flowers and vegetables. Lavender *(Lavandula officinalis)* is an ornamental and medicinal shrub that comes from the Mediterranean. Anciently introduced, thyme *(Thymus sp.),* a medicinal and culinary herb, is both native and from the Mediterranean. A number of varieties and species were grown, including the lemon-scented type. Chives *(Allium schoenoprasum)* and mints *(Menta sp.)* were culinary and medicinal in use and were native. A dozen or so species and hybrids were known and used. Rosemary *(Rosmarinus officinalis)* is a medicinal, culinary and ornamental shrub from the Mediterranean. Basil *(Ocimum basilicum),* used medicinally and for culinary purposes, was from

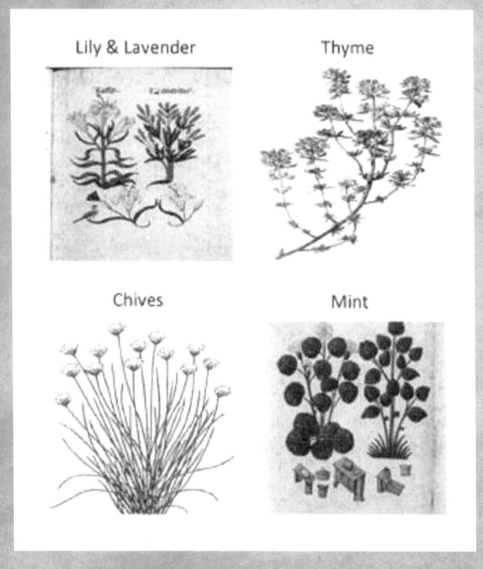

Fig. 5 Other Vegetation. Lavender[15] and Mints[16] retrieved from ARTstor, Manuscripts and Early Printed Books. These medieval images can be found at the Bodleian Library at the University Of Oxford, England. Herbs including Thyme[17] and Chives[18] obtained from Google Images.

Asia. Another featured prominently was saffron *(Crocus sativus)*, with the stigmas from the flowers used as spice, cosmetics, and dye. Saffron bulbs were occasionally used medicinally; native to Asia Minor, they had been introduced by the Romans. Sage *(Salvia officinalis)* was a culinary and medicinal herb from the Mediterranean. What is more, on the word of Thomas Hill in *The Gardener's Labyrinth,* "Sage may be sowed of seeds, but the best way is to set the slips in spring". [Hill 96] These are some of the herbs that were used to decorate gardens in Elizabethan designs. Also, these herbs usually spread some fragrance within the garden.[19]

Additionally, vegetables from Asia were cultivated for medicinal uses, such as garlic *(Allium sativum)*. Anciently introduced to Britain, beans *(Leguminous)* were from Europe and Asia. Some dozen different varieties were in cultivation in England in the sixteenth-century, including broad and tick beans and an increasing number of kidney and "runner" beans from the New World. The young pods of these were cooked and eaten whole, exactly as today, but the showier varieties were also grown as ornamental climbers. Onions *(Allium cepa)* from Central Asia were probably introduced by the Romans. Varieties grown included the scallion or shallot, and the winter, spring, or Welsh onion, and they were often used as extra decorations in the gardens.[Hill 10-17]

Despite all the new introductions during this time, the garden at Kenilworth remained medieval in many respects. The tunnel arbors and statues consisted of Dudley's bears and show that Elizabethan gardens were not complete without a display of statues around them.[Martyn 104] Sometimes a simple decorative pot could be used, while at other times complex water fountains could dot the garden. In addition, Elizabethan aesthetics relied heavily on the blending of architecture and outdoor spaces in their gardens. The central idea of these gardens was relaxation and enjoyment. Archaeologists have found inventory records drawn up by the Parliamentary Surveyors in 1649 that lists a "Queen's seat of freestone," which stood in the garden.[Martyn 106] Special stone or wooden benches could be situated at places inside the garden to allow for some vantage points for the various aesthetic dimensions of the garden.

The Kenilworth Castle Garden

Apart from seeking to please the queen through the pompous gardening, Dudley also sought to illustrate his worth and social standing to convince the queen of the merits of his romantic quest. The size and designs of Elizabethan gardens illustrated the social standing of the owners. The lofty design of the garden at the Kenilworth castle was, therefore, meant to both endear Dudley to the queen and to convince the royal family of the suitability of Dudley settling into the privileged role of the queen's husband. His intention was to illustrate his admiration for the Queen by lavishing the grounds around the castle with artistic designs like the terrace and obelisk that have often been called extravagant. The gardening was specifically created to give the place an air of ceremony and power.

The geometrical angles[20] of the building side of the Kenilworth Castle garden express in traditional English terms ideals of beauty. Further, the Elizabethans delighted in devices and strategy. This was shown in their castle architecture, employing geometric patterns, letters and symbols in their plans, decorative work, and gardens. Thus their constructions, including gardens, often have hidden meanings. The queen is said to have visited the Kenilworth Castle gardens at least four times[21] in her lifetime, and all these while celebrating the lavish designs of the garden. Dudley spared no expense for Elizabeth's last visit in 1575; lasting 19 days, it is reputed to have cost him $1000 per day ($190,000 as of 2010),[22] an amount that nearly caused bankruptcy.[Gardens in Warwickshire 11]

Private Garden for the Queen - Kenilworth Castle

The garden represents the intentions of Dudley as a man who would be king, while establishing the hallmarks of Renaissance character that emerged during the Tudor era. The Garden may be seen as an effort by Leicester to represent his regal qualities, from accentuating his noble stature with heraldic imprints on garden surfaces, to demonstrating - in the aviary and fountain - his ability to impose his power over the natural world. His efforts to convince Elizabeth of his matrimonial worth may have proved a failure, but the garden has become a Symbol of the age and an illustration of the influence Renaissance elements had on Leicester, Elizabeth, and appreciation of the Tudor period.

Fig 6. Queen Elizabeth I and Robert Dudley. Obtained from media storehouse
id 1647171 www.mediastorehouse.com

In many ways, Dudley seems to have been predestined to build the garden at Kenilworth. As a youth, he received ample training in both Latin and Italian, then considered to be languages for the privileged.[(Woodhouse 128)] He was made Lord Protector of the young queen in 1562 and was rewarded with numerous houses and estates, most notably Kenilworth, which had been in his family's lineage previously.[(Haynes 12)]

Queen Elizabeth honored Dudley with a visit in 1565. It was a visit a decade later that inspired Dudley, now Earl of Leicester, to build a garden to entice Elizabeth to marry him. The garden, described in a letter by Robert Laneham (sometimes written Langham[23]), may be seen as the centerpiece of the manor grounds and expressed through symbolism the desires that Leicester could not say to the queen outright. A man worthy of being a king must come from a noble lineage. The Dudley power originated not very long before, during the reign of Henry VII, when Edmund Dudley, Robert's grandfather, served as financial minister.[(Jenkins 7)] Robert's father John, Duke of Northumberland, found favor with Henry VIII and held several posts in the court.[(8-9)] To establish his credentials, Robert used the garden's heraldic[24] features to remind his royal visitor of his ancestry.

Dudley's personal profile and demeanor suggest a man who was extremely class conscious. Certain personal devices, symbols, and artifacts, such as cinquefoils (a five-leaved clover or five petalled flower form, within a red circle), were carefully chosen to illustrate a desire for immortality. In the garden's design, circles with squares represented "eternity within mortality, body and soul or heaven upon earth".[(Martyn 80)] This same deportment and behavior prodded him into the bold attempt to seduce and attempt to marry the queen whom he had adored and served since childhood. [(Woodhouse 128)] Further, Dudley used figures of bears to recall his heritage and express the power of great animals as well as their renowned habit of waking from a period of long sleep. A stone statue of a white bear in chains stands on a pedestal on the terrace overlooking the garden, and sculptural forms of white bears made of stone were situated along the terrace.

As the Renaissance reached England, Leicester's garden reinforced many of its themes. The idea of combining artistic elements with or in nature is a Renaissance ideal,[(Woodhouse 127)] and in Leicester's case, the additional suggestion that he could tame the natural world made the garden as a whole more emblematic. Dudley made it a point to moderate his work with varieties of art borrowed from different cultures across Europe, drawing from the various cultural influences that entered Europe through the efforts of explorers and emperors. Small by Renaissance standards, Leicester's garden adds depth by its inclusion of a raised, grass-covered terrace (perhaps the first of its kind in England) and by the inclusion of obelisks. Each porphyry obelisk was topped by a sphere. These forms reflected the Renaissance fascination with ancient Egypt art and were also emblems of Robert Dudley. An obelisk encircled by a vine provided a code for his love[25] of Elizabeth dating back to a tilt-yard tournament the day after her coronation.[(Martyn 17)] The entertainment that he commissioned for Elizabeth's visit may have promoted not just the idea of marriage, but his own hopes of leading an army, in that they showed women in jeopardy and in need of rescue by a protective masculinity.[26] The Laneham Letter description includes the comment that Dudley spent a fortune on the garden and showpiece event.[(Laneham 48)]

Architecture

The Kenilworth garden was designed to illustrate the aristocratic traditions of the upper class in the sixteenth-century British tradition. The grounds were decorated with a planting scheme that exuded bright color, rich perfume, and fruit. Arguably, the Kenilworth garden is one of the gardens that illustrate the most supreme depictions of the standards that defined the Elizabethan aesthetic. (Laneham 31-33)

The garden was a rectangular enclosure with magnificent carved arbors, a high fountain, and a bejeweled aviary. The essence of this planning was to astound visitors, most particularly, the beloved Queen Elizabeth I. The concentration of the floral allure of the garden is mostly represented in the right-hand court. This was the part designed for entertainment, while the backgrounds (the woods) were meant for hunting. The base court (out of the east arbor) also carried several square knot gardens. A knot garden is a type of English garden design which developed during the reign of Queen Elizabeth I. The formal design was usually grown using a variety of herbs, such as thyme, rosemary, and others, which were grown in hedges forming a cluster. The hedges were often separated by paths of gravel. The private garden was designed with a steep terrace on the south side along with elaborate steps leading down to eight-square knot gardens. (Laneham 33)

Elizabethan gardens were constructed with limited plantations, as most designers seemed to concentrate on the sculptures. In its original form, Kenilworth Castle garden borrowed much of its design from Italian garden architecture, such as the Renaissance garden at Villa d' Este,[27] although with some modifications to suit British culture. One such modification included Dudley's trick fountain, referred to as "water jokes" and showed his sense of humor. (Martyn 102) Further, Dudley's patronage of Frederico Zuccaro suggests that Kenilworth was modeled on Cardinal Gambara's garden at Villa Lante, at Bagnaia in Lazio. At the Villa Lante, Giacomo da Vignola used geometry and terraces to create illusions of space. Borrowing from this tradition at Kenilworth, the architecture formed a single, unified landscape including the garden, park, woods, lake, and castle, all designed to be viewed as a whole. (Martyn 101)

One of the historically notable features of the Kenilworth Castle garden was the spot of Pleasance, an earthwork situated on the north-west of the castle. Desiring to increase the anachronistic effect of the castle's appearance (before Elizabeth's reign), Henry VIII removed the Pleasance and transferred it to the left-hand court in the interior of the castle. It was a banqueting house designed to appear like a small castle. Around the spot of Pleasance were two diamond-shaped moats with their own dock. It was located at a distance from the Great Mere[28] and could only be reached by boat.

The preferred route that tourists would take on their maiden trip to the Kenilworth Castle Palace was the same route usually used by Elizabeth on her 1575 tour. Dudley transformed the site by making the north entrance the main entrance. He also added the Leicester building, a

Fig. 7 Kenilworth Castle. Obtained from media storehouse id 1634417
www.mediastorehouse.com

large apartment and residential block overlooking the lake.[Gardens in Warwickshire 11] Elizabeth may have caught her first peek at the garden from a small Italianate courtyard which Dudley fitted alongside the Norman keep. She would then have moved down steps within the wall, emerging between the heraldic bears of Leicester's crest to the high terrace.[Mawrey and Groves 14] The loggia of the castle's fore-building leads to the facility's terrace deliberately made large to create a feel of royal power. The terrace affords the first-time visitor with the fullest view of the facility, including all dimensions of the landscape.

Some of the most conspicuous attractions of the gardens are the obelisks, Leicester symbols, and spheres stylistically placed at different locations of the garden. The obelisk that

Fig. 8 Kenilworth Castle Elizabethan Garden. Obtained from media storehouse
id 1991311 www.mediastorehouse.com

stands up to 17 feet was traditionally used as a symbol of power and leadership. Although they appear to be of porphyry, they were most likely made of painted wood to appear as such, in view of the fact that no porphyry has been found during the most recent archeological digs. (Mawrey and Groves 14)

The Bear

The best observation of the garden is from the terrace where the Earl of Leicester's standard. "The Bear with ragged staff", rests on pedestals. An arbor on each end envelope the stairways leading into the garden. When the Leicester family assumed the Warwick title, its heraldic representation became the white bear and the ragged staff, which was a main heraldic image of the Elizabethan period. With regard to the Warwick title. we find that by merging the past and present;... "Earl of Leicester, favourite of Queen Elizaberh I, and great-great-great- grandson of Richard Beauchamp, is know n to have used the combined device of the bear and ragged staff frequently. It can be seen in many places on the walls of the Leicester Hospital in Warwick, which he founded in 1571, and on chimney piece in his castle of Kenilworth. "(Warwickshire)

Although the origins of these emblems were lost in the times of yore, they are generally associated with the earls of Warwick at least as early as the 14th century. William Dugdale's writings of the 1650s said that Arthgal, an Earl of Warwick at the time of King Arthur thought that his name came from the Welsh "artos" or bear. He also suggested that the ragged staff was chose because Morvidus, Earl of Warwick, killed a giant with the broken branch of a tree.

However, this information is perceptibly more fable than fact.

Later, Robert Dudley, the Earl of Leicester, was branded in court circles as "The Bear". In The Ruines of Time, Spenser praises the Earls of Warwick and Leicester as "two bears, as white as anie milke,/... Two fairer beasts might not elswherebe found,/ Although the compass world were sought around.(Spencer) Further, an expanded account of the restoration of the garden including the emblematic sign is provided by Ind. English Heritage, which now manages the castle, undertook a meticulous investigation of the site and discovered that the archaeological proof matched with Langham's descriptions.

Lanham said the garden was an acre in size. The archaeological findings backed this up. And he gave the precise location of an eight sided fountain, the foundations of which were found through the digging. "The Letter says it was white marble from the Carrara quarry in Italy. We found chips of marble during the excavation and it was confirmed they were from the fountain and that particular quarry in Italy,"...having gasped at the fountain, which is huge and ornate and carved with scenes from Ovid ... to a 21st century eye, it looks garish and distasteful. Upon observing them, Langham said: "Here were things, ye see, might inflame any mind to long after look ... "Dudley was evidently aware that such raunchiness might get his queen going and so had created a little water point nearby "with water spurting upward with so much vehemency, as they should, by and by, be moistening from top to toe" they could cool off afterwards. "One of the hardest things to communicate how it might have appeared to an Elizabethan," says Tamsin Rosewell a member of the English Heritage team at Kenilworth. "I would regard it was an emblematic garden. If you were an Elizabethan you would walk into the garden and almost be able to read it like a book. It is full of the Earl of Leicester's heraldic symbols. At this period of history, you might well expect to find a garden that glorified Elizabeth I, but what we found is a garden that glorified the Earl of Leicester, with the bears and the ragged staff at the top of the fountain. This is all to do with his family heraldry and what he seems to be doing is positioning himself as somebody of high aristocracy."

The English Heritage team endeavoured to be as historically accurate as possible, but drew the line at cramming more than 200 birds into the aviary, as would have happened in ELizabethan days.[Ind]

What is more as a patron of the arts, drama and literature, the Earl of Leicester displayed as much of the representative heraldry as possible with regard to his old and powerful lineage:

"His Garden featured his emblem of a bear and ragged staff (and sometimes cinquefoils) on every conceivable surface.

"The bear... was the symbol of Mores Occulti or concealed habits- returning to life when circumstances became favourable',"[Woodhouse]

It is interesting that more findings and research with regard to these heraldic symbols of the Elizabethan Era are becoming increasingly known:

> Dudley's association with the bear motif would have been familiar to a large part of society. In addition to the publicity he would have inevitably received when he was awarded the Garter, he would have been particularly well known figure within the theatre going community because of his patronage of the Earl's Men. And within educated, literate society, I believe he received further significant publicity through Geffrey Whitney's Choice of Emblems (1586). The book bore a dedication to him, and the bearish crest was printed in full on its second page.[Holmes]

It is certainly not at all surprising that emblematical and heraldic bears would have been included, several times in the Earl of Leicester's legendary gardens.

The latest empirical research and scientific conclusions on Elizabethan Era gardens have hold a significant impact. Regardless of the reason, the authors of previous works on this period type of garden have created an even larger culture to gain a more prolific audience. They have completed this by including tables of information, illustrations, correspondence, art works and many other pieces of gardening information for readers. Previous investigations plus recent findings and archaeological digs at Kenilworth Castle grounds, have provided for important solutions to the problem of the lost gardens of the Elizabethan Era. It is critical to note, that, to date Kenilworth Castle Gardens is understood to be the only accurately restored Elizabethan Era garden in existence.

The Fountain in the Garden

The fountain at the Kenilworth garden was made of Carrara marble with eight sides.[29] It is unclear whether the eight sides alluded to some medieval or biblical creations. It was situated at the center, so that visitors walking about the garden could not fail to see it. Water from the fountain is believed to have risen up to 18 feet high, so it was one of the primary art forms that shaped the skyline of the magnificent garden. The octagonal base is ornamented with what appear, at first glance, as erotic scenes. Fish swam in the basin, while two Atlantes support a sphere from which water was sprayed from "sundry pipes." This sphere is topped by a "ragged" staff, yet another heraldic symbol from Leicester's crest.[(Mawrey and Groves 14)] The fountain would resonate with the rhythm of peace and tranquility usually associated with the aristocratic life and creates an ambience above normal reality so that a heavenly allure was created.

The water from the fountain gave a natural rhythm to the garden, so the bustle of everyday life was effectively blocked out of the imagination of the beholder. Elizabethan aesthetic values were made to reflect aspects of naturalism in a way that painted the age as particularly heavenly. In the strict Elizabethan tradition, royalty was conceptualized as a form of ordination, and the occupants of the throne were regarded in terms that suggested their close links with God. The imagination that yielded the form and structure of the garden would be naturally made to evoke this relationship between the monarchy and Godliness.

The creative impulse that governed the aesthetics of the garden was also sourced from classical poetry. Famous Greek poetic works such as the **Iliad** and **Odyssey** by Homer and the Roman poet Ovid's **Metamorphoses** were some of the imaginative sources that can be seen through in the creative substance of the garden. The eight scenes that form the panels around the basin of the fountain portray scenes from Ovid. Ovid's literature explores the theme of transformation of man into animals and plants. This represents the Elizabethan impulses that delved into the questions of transition, mortality, and providence, all gods associated with water. Other Greco-Roman gods alluded to in this garden fountain are Doris, Triton, and Neptune. With the fountain basin full of fish such as carp, tench, bream, perch, and eels, the scenes show Neptune on his throne, driving his marine horses and Thetis in her chariot drawn by dolphins would seem naturally linked.[(Martyn 81)]

The obvious attempt to situate the artistic elements of the garden around Greco-Roman classical mythology was Dudley's gesture of forging the Elizabethan values of love into mythical proportions. The discourse of love in the Greek mythological structure was captured in heavy allusions that moved in and outside the boundaries of man and nature and the gods.[(Woodhouse 127)] This certainly shows his attempts to appeal to the beloved queen on the basis of the scope, magnitude, and dimension of his love for her.

Aviaries were commonly used in English Renaissance art, although they were borrowed from French culture. The birds that were kept were mostly captured wild birds, although some domestic varieties could also be kept. The Kenilworth Castle garden aviary was a 30-foot (9m) structure made in the classical style containing exotic birds perching on clipped holly bushes, including colorful birds from the Canary Islands,[Martyn 82] others imported from the mainland, and some from possibly as far away as Africa.[Mawrey and Groves 15] Dudley preferred to keep some of the wild birds that he had captured in his hunting jaunts in the background of the garden. The situation in the modern British culture has, however, changed much, mainly because environmentalists and lobbyists have pushed for legislation against the taming of wild birds. The Kenilworth garden's aviary was situated alongside the alluring floral sections of the garden for the purpose of completing the exquisite picturesque of the garden. The use of the aviary, with the extensive mix of wild and domestic birds, might allude to the imperialist intentions of the Elizabethan period.

Precious stones (or their imitation) were used in the framework of the aviary to complement the aesthetics of the garden, although their actual import was to create a feeling of affluence so that the aristocratic qualities that were naturally represented in royalty were effectively captured. The most commonly used stones during the Elizabethan era were emeralds, sapphires, and rubies. The use of precious stones elevated Dudley's status. Dudley's almost extravagant use of these stones was meant to situate himself strategically on the social ladder as a man of immense wealth and capability.

How to Re-Create Kenilworth Castle Garden

Efforts to recreate Kenilworth garden have resulted in misrepresentations by artists and gardeners. Many of the gardeners who endeavored to re-create this garden have revised some of the structural forms desired by its Elizabethan creators. The most probable reason for these historical distortions might be the desire to remodel the Elizabethan traditions according to contemporary ideas of beautification. When this happens, the qualities that were espoused in the Elizabethan traditions of aesthetics get distorted. With a plan to maintain the best of the past and enable potential assets for the future to be generated, the restoration of the Kenilworth Castle garden was made possible with an opening in 2009.[Mawrey and Groves 10]

Shifts in ideological structures of the various artists and gardeners have also meant that the garden conforms to the realities of the different times, thereby losing the authentic qualities designed by its most potent creator, Dudley. There have been efforts by historians, however, to return the garden to its structural identity by re-creating the values that defined the aesthetics of Elizabethan period. It is nevertheless difficult to reconstruct the Elizabethan garden fully. What are available are fragmented pieces of knowledge that are mostly based on the archaeological facts and ideological interpretations.

The boldest attempt to re-create the Kenilworth Castle garden was by English heritage after careful archaeological investigations. The objective was to re-build the garden, as accurately as possible, in line with the sights and sounds as they appeared over 400 years ago.[Corbett] The structural symbols of the Elizabethan times had to be re-created following the authentic forms so as to achieve the classical rhythm of art that alone can record the art form of the Kenilworth garden.

Recreating this garden must originate from the vivid descriptions offered in the writings of Robert Laneham, one of the few characters who was privileged with inside details of the aesthetics of the Elizabethan Kenilworth garden. The picturesque image that the new creators must emphasize should be one that evokes the racy and lavish descriptions of Laneham. The process of re-creating the Kenilworth castle garden must begin with a group of dedicated professionals of the best availability that are sympathetic to period style gardens as well as historic preservation. Ideally, the hiring of an assemblage of stone masons, accomplished carpenters, and master sculptors would be key to the project, funding permitted. Some of the prominent features that this team will have to work on are the bejeweled aviary arbors and heraldic symbols. Other features that must receive special attention are carved arbors, perfumed plants and obelisks. Competent gardeners should then re-create the wild strawberries (alpine varieties), pear trees, and other floral lawns in the precise dimension as were illustrated in the Elizabethan tradition. At the center of the garden, the creators should put a carved marble fountain which should rise to a height of about 18 feet so that it looks almost exactly like its authentic form.

The sculptors should take special care in re-creating the sensual scenes around the basin of the fountain so that the exact form of Ovid's **Metamorphoses** is not confused with some of other antique sculptures, as has sometimes happened. Careful creation of the scenes will help achieve the symbolic effect as imagined by Dudley, when he fancied the gushing water as cooling the sculptural forms that seem to be hot in carnal desire.

The mapping of this garden should agree with the archaeological findings of 2004 and 2006. This must include accuracy in sizes and shapes of the art forms and the geometry that underline the structural form of the garden. This should include the use of white marble for the fountain as in the original form. Special focus should be taken to present the decoration in the most sensational of ways so that it retains the original meaning. The picturesque result should be romanticized and captured in creative connotations that situate it in the regal context as desired by Dudley when he created it more than 400 years ago. Special attention must be taken to exclude all aspects of more recent art that might have the effect of distorting the Elizabethan aspects of beauty. The flowers used in the re-created garden must include only those that were actually used in the Elizabethan garden.

Special care must be taken to capture the fragrances and beauty of the cherries and strawberries. The birds to be used in the aviaries must all be exotic, although a little revision and modification might have to be done on the aviaries to accommodate modern laws that outlaw the caging of wild birds. Wild birds should, however, be retained within the hunting sections of the garden in great variety, so that what is lost in the aviaries is sufficiently compensated in the forest section of the garden. Precaution should be taken fencing the garden so that it does not appear to shift to conventional standards against the forms and substance of the sixteenth century.

The flowers and plant types should be arranged with edible types on one side and inedible fruit types on the opposite side of the garden. The use of rectangular forms should be the preferred setup since the historical garden carried the same aspects. This arrangement should be repeated with other forms of plants around the recreated garden. Moreover, strictly follow the evidence obtained through your own research and/or the background set in the preceding text.

There are still few verifiable and actual accounts of Elizabethan era gardens due to the destruction during the civil war after her death in 1603. Any successful re-creation of the example of the Kenilworth garden, used in this handbook, must strike a delicate balance between the conflicting accounts of features as reflected in all available works. The majesty of royal life and the historical aspects of the Elizabethan garden should be captured in logical detail of flora, fauna, and sculpture as celebrated in the sixteenth-century Kenilworth castle garden.

Notes

1. An article in the English newspaper *Independent* noted: "It's been a long haul for English Heritage, who took over responsibility for the castle in 1984. A 'Tudor' garden, based on a 1656 map (erroneous as it turned out) had been laid out in the Seventies, with yew topiary and box-edged beds. It was thought to be excellent and won awards. But by the Eighties, the same processes that archaeologists use on ancient sites were beginning to be used in historic gardens. Geophysical surveys revealed the hidden remains of Dudley's garden, deep underground. The Seventies garden was in the wrong place. And research had now shown that topiaried yew wasn't used in Elizabethan gardens. Worse, the roots of the newly introduced yews were breaking up the underground remains of the original garden" http://www.independent.co.uk/life-style/houseand- home/gardening/kenilworth-castle-gardens-have-undergone-a-major-restoration-thanks-tohightech-surveying-ndash-and-a-remarkable-16thcentury-letter-1716999.html. See also, Woodhouse, Elisabeth. "Kenilworth, the Earl of Leicester's Pleasure Grounds Following Robert Langham's Letter." Garden History 27.1 (1999) and Martyn, Trea. Elizabeth in the Garden. London. Faber and Faber Limited, 2008.

2. Consider "Sir Philip Sidney (30 November 1554 - 17 October 1586) 'who' became one of the Elizabethan Age's most prominent figures. Famous in his day in England as a poet, courtier and soldier, he remains to be known as the author of **Astrophel and Stella** (1581, pub. 1591), **The Defence of Poetry** (also known as The Defence of Poesy or An Apology for poetry, 1581, pub. 1595), and **The Countess of pembroke's Arcadia** (1580, pub. 1590)" http://www.web.tv/.

3. By way of example review local histories perspective: "In the 16th century there was a revival of the ideas of ancient Greece and Rome. Ideas about gardening changed and were influenced by classical ideas" http://www.localhistories.org/gardening.html.

4. One source suggests that "To the outward eye there was very little difference in her treatment of the handsome and daring nobles of her court, yet a historian of her time makes one very shrewd remark when he says: 'To everyone she gave some power at times-to all save Leicester'" http://www.authorama.comlfamous-affinities-of-history-i-3.html.

5. Bear in mind that "In the 16th century, England was a poor country. When they began colonizing, it was not as missionaries. When the English put to sea, it aimed to seek immediate profits" http://www.skwirk.com.au/p-c_s-17_u-504_t-1362_c-5243/great-britain/qld/greatbritain/colonisation- resources-power-and-exploration/colonisation-history.

6. During the Elizabethan era "Landscape gardens also carried a certain political message. Early on, they were identified with British liberalism, distaste for tyranny and autocracy, and reliance upon home-grown aesthetics, as opposed to foreign influences" http://gardendesigns. inrebus.com.

7. Interestingly, "Elizabethans loved anything with colour and if it had scent, all the better. The scent comes mainly from the carnations which have since been bred out, but we have tried to get old-fashioned varieties. They smell so heavily of cinnamon and cloves - heady scents that attracted the Elizabethans, which is exactly what we have tried to re-create" http://www.iog.org/latest_news_and_media/articles-of-interest/grounds_and_surfaces/Kenilworth+Castle.

8. Keep in mind that "The Tudor rose and the queen's motto of 'Semper Eadem,' along with its symbolic equivalent of the reborn Phoenix rising from its own ashes" provide the core essence of this icon. (King 70)

9. We see this point advanced in the following quote "of so many God's blessings, by entire delight unto all senses (if all can take) at once; for etymon of the word worthy to be called Paradise: and though not so goodly as Paradise, for want of the fair rivers, yet better a great deal by the lack of so unhappy a tree. Argument most certain of a right noble mind, that in this sort could have thus all contrived. - Letter describing the Pageants at Kenilworth Castle, 1575" http://www.archive.org/stream/gardensancienta00sievgoog/gardensancienta00sievgoog_djvu.txt.

10. Woodcut acquired from "The Illustrated Bartsch." Vol. 90, German Book of Illustration through 1500: Herbals through 1500. Bodleian Library, University of Oxford. (1520-1530). Image. ARTstor, Manuscripts and Early Printed Books.

11. Ceramic, polychrome dish was acquired from "The Tudor Pattern Book." Trans. Durer and etc the grotesque alphabet of 1464. East Anglia? Bodleian Library, University of Oxford. (1520-1530). Image. ARTstor, Manuscripts and Early Printed Books.

12. Manuscript (paper) acquired from "The Tudor Pattern Book." Trans. Durer and etc the grotesque alphabet of 1464. East Anglia? Bodleian Library, University of Oxford. (1520-1530). Image. ARTstor, Manuscripts and Early Printed Books.

13. Woodcut (published 23 June 1491) acquired from "The Illustrated Bartsch." Vol. 90, German Book of Illustration through 1500: Herbals through 1500. Bodleian Library, University of Oxford. (1520-1530). Image. ARTstor, Manuscripts and Early Printed Books.

14. Get the picture "Unsigned Engraving from Michael Friedrich Lochner (1662-1720) **Michaelis Friderici Lochneri ... Nerium, sive, Rhododaphne veterum et recentiorum ...** Nuremberg: J. Hoffmanni, 1716 Citrus trees as well as other exotic, rare or tender plants such as Oleander, were planted in tubs or decorative pots. **Nerium oleander** is native to the Mediterranean region and was the only kind of Oleander known in Europe until 1683 when Rheede Tot Drakenstein introduced in Holland a cultivated oleander from India" Image.

15. Parchment in manuscript form entitled: Lily and Lavender. Birds, two lilies, moth. Copied partly from German models (Durer, the grotesque alphabet of 1464, etc.). Contains the arms of John de Vere, Earl of Oxford, d. 1513, and of the Emperor Charles V (after 1519). Ashmole1504 ro1l156B frame20.

16. Parchment in manuscript form entitled: Mallow and Mint. Stool, 3 baskets, book-stand, prie-dieu, cupboard. Copied partly from German models (Durer, the grotesque alphabet of 1464, etc.). Contains the arms of John de Vere, Earl of Oxford, d. 1513, and of the Emperor Charles V (after 1519). Ashmolel504, ro1l156B, frame23. Illustration acquired from "The Tudor Pattern Book." Trans. Durer and etc the grotesque alphabet of 1464. East Anglia? Bodleian Library, University of Oxford. (1520-1530). Image. **ARTstor, Manuscripts and Early Printed Books.**

17. Thyme obtained from **Google Images** searching illustrations from United Kingdom before 1603.

18. Chives obtained from **Google Images** searching drawings from United Kingdom before 1603.

19. Laneham's letter about Queen Elizabeth I's visit to Kenilworth castle in 1575 puts it: "Redolent plants and fragrant herbs and flowers, in form, colour and quantity so deliciously variant, and fruit-trees bedecked with their apples, pears and ripe cherries". [(Laneham 50)]

20. Think about the fact that "The master mason was an important figure in medieval society. He was responsible for the selection of the stone, supervision of the masons, and also the design and the "setting out" of levels, angles and dimensions of the building" http://www.englishstone.org.uk/documents/Building%20stone%20for%20teachers.pdf.

21. It is believed that "Elizabeth visited Dudley at Kenilworth Castle several times in 1566, 1568, 1572 and 1575". [(Gardens in Warwickshire 11)]

22. Take into account "UK CPI inflation numbers based on data available from Measuring Worth: UK CPI"[(Gardens in Warwickshire 12)]

23. We are dependent on "Robert Langham, a former London mercer who held a post as gentleman-usher to Leicester. Although ostensibly addressed to a friend, Humfrey Martyn, the letter was almost certainly intended for publication - or at least for circulation amongst the gentry in London - and Leicester was most likely aware of its contents, so flattering to his person, his garden and his ambition"[(Martyn 16)]

24. During that time, "Heraldry is both a science and an art form. Developing out of the emblems and insignia born upon shields and banners during battle, heraldry as a profession encompasses not only the devising, granting, and blazoning of arms, but also the tracing of genealogies, and determining and ruling on questions of rank or protocol"[(University of Notre Dame)]

25. Evocatively "Dudley also had a shield showing an obelisk with a vine entwined around it - code for his love for Elizabeth. The Latin motto beneath translated: 'You standing I will flourish'"[Martyn 17].

26. Persuasively, "One historian has noted that the entertainments Leicester commissioned tended to promote not only marriage, but militarism - his own hopes of leading an army to the Netherlands; that they tended to show women in jeopardy, in need of being rescued by a protective masculinity". [Gristwood 248]

27. Martyn gives historical credibility to her research when she associates that "The concept of the garden designer as architect and engineer originated in Italy; in the case of the gardens of the Villa d'Este, the designer, Pirro Ligorio, was also an archaeologist inspired by the remains of Roman pleasure grounds and a scholar of classical literature and mythology". [Martyn 38]

28. Soon after "After the civil war, parliamentarians drained the Great Mere, and the fertile acres left behind have been used for agriculture ever since". [Mawrey and Groves 15]

29. See further "Brian Dix, Brian Kerr and Joe Prentice, 'Archaeology' in Anna Keay and John Watkins[ids], 'Worthy to be Called Paradise': Re-Creating the Elizabethan Garden at Kenilworth Castle (London: English Heritage, forthcoming)". [Dix]

Works Cited

"Book of Hours." (1513). Image. *ARTstor, Manuscripts and Early Printed Books.* 12 May 2011

Corbett, Anthony. *Kenilworth Castle.* 5 January 2003. <http://www.celcat.com/kworth/castle. html>.

Corrie, Roger. *Kenilworth Castle.* 31 July 1835. <http://www.history.rochester.edu/ pennymag/213/castle.htm#a>.

Dix, Brian. "Experiencing the past: the archaeology of some Renaissance gardens." *Renaissance Studies* (n.d.): 162-165.

King, John. "Queen Elizabeth I: Representations of the Virgin Queen." *Renaissance Quarterly* (1990): 70.

English Heritage. *Kenilworth Castle,* "The Privy Garden Plant List" London: English Heritage, printed by Hawthomes, 2009.

Gardens in Warwickshire:Kenilworth Castle, Warwick Castle, the Jephson Gardens, Ragley Hall, Packwood House, Charlecote Park, Upton House. Memphis: Books LLC, 2010.

Haynes, Alan. *The White Bear: Robert Dudley, the Elizabethan Earl of Leicester.* London: Peter Owen, 1987.

Hill, Thomas, and Richard Mabey. *The Gardener's Labyrinth.* Oxford. [Oxfordshire]: New York: Oxford University Press, 1987.

Holmes, Chris. *"A Bear Necessity?: The significance of the ursine protagonist in the year of 1611."* 2005. http://zoohistory.co.uk/htm/modules/Downloads/files/abearnecessity.pdf

"The Illustrated Bartsch." Vol. 90, German Book of Illustration through 1500: Herbals through 1500. Image. *ARTstor, Manuscripts and Early Printed Books.* 12 May 2011

Ind. Jo "The Birmingham Post: A garden tit to woo a queen." *The (England) Birmingham Post.* 1 May 2009.

Jenkins, Elizabeth. *Elizabeth and Leicester.* New York: Coward-Mccann, 1962.

King, John N. "Queen Elizabeth I: representations of the Virgin Queen" *Renaissance Quarterly,* 43.1 (1990): 30+.

Laneham, Robert. *Laneham's Letter Describing The Magnificent Pageants Presented Before Queen Elizabeth, At Kenilworth Castle In 1575.* London: J.H. Burn, 2009.

Lanham, Robert and Frederick James Furnival. *Robert Laneham's Letter: Describing a Part of the Entertainment Unto Queen Elizabeth at the Castle of Kenilworth in 1575.* London: Chatto and Windus, 1907.

Martyn, Trea. *Elizabeth in the Garden.* London: Faber and Faber Limited, 2008.

Mawrey, Gillian and Linden Groves. *The Gardens of English Heritage.* London: Frances Lincoln Limited, 2010.

National Garden Clubs, Inc. *Handbook For Flower Shows, Growing & Designing, Staging & Exhibiting, Judging.* National Garden Clubs. St. Louis, 2007.

Spencer, Edmund and Henry John Todd. *The Works of Edmund Spencer: With a Selection of Notes from Various Commentators; and a Glossarial Index: To Which Is Prefixed, Some Account of the Life of Spencer, by Henry John Todd.* Toronto: Nabu Press, 2010.

"The Tudor Pattern Book." Trans. Durer and etc the grotesque alphabet of 1464. East Angria? Bodleian Library, University of Oxford. (1520-1530). Image. *ARTstor, Manuscripts and Early Printed Books.*

University of Notre Dame. *Heraldic Dictionary.* 31 July 2010. <http://www.rarebooks.nd.edu/digital/heraldry/>.

Warwickshire Museum and County Record Office. *Bear and Ragged Staff.* 23 June 2010. http://www.warwickshire.gov.uk/web/corporate/pages.nsf/Links2AA8F37EFE001B180256A38003531A9

Woodhouse, Elisabeth. *"Kenilworth, the Earl of Leicester's Pleasure Grounds Following Robert Langham's Letter."* Garden History 27.1 (1999): 127-144.

Woodhouse, Elisabeth. *"Kenilworth, the Earl of Leicester's Pleasure."* JSTOR. The Garden Society. Summer 1999. Web. 17 Sept. 2010. http://www.jstor.org/stable/1587177.

Further Reading

Abbott, Jane. *Being A Compendium Of Knowledge Historical And Practical About Flowers Of The Elizabethan Age For Use By The Modern Gardener.* Flowers for An Elizabethan Garden. <http://home.netcom.corn! ~janeabbt/flowers/welcome.html>.

Alchin, L.K. *Elizabethan Era.* <http://www.elizabethanera.org.uk>.

Anderton, Stephen. "A Garden Fit for a Queen,' Made for Elizabeth I, the Garden at Kenilworth Castle Has Been Re-created after 400 Years, Says Stephen Anderton." *Times* [London, England].

Andrews, Martin. "Theobalds Palace: The Gardens and Park." Garden History Society. 21.2 1993: 129-149.

Aspden, Peter A. *"A Garden Fit for a Queen."*, <http://find.galegroup.com/gtx/infomark. do?&contentSet=lAC->.

Beck, Thomasina. "Gardens in Elizabethan Embroidery." *Garden History Society.* 3.1 1974: 44-56.

Brooks, Richard, ed. "Bickering Blooms in a Queen's Garden: A [pound Sterling]3m RESTORATION PROJECT IS BESET BY FEUDING." *Sunday Times* [London, England].

Brown, Richard. *Domestic Architecture: Containing a History of the Science, and the Principles Of Designing Public Edifices, Private Dwelling-houses ... With Some Observations on Rural Residences, Their Situation and Scenery,' and Instructions on the Art of Laying out and Imbellishing Grounds.* Google Books. G. Virtue, 1841,2010.

Butterfield, Bruce. "Survey Reveals Double-Digit Increase in Food Gardening for 2009." "Reuters National Gardening Association."

Burton, Elizabeth. *The Pageant of Elizabethan England.* New York: Scribner, 1959.

Davis, Alex. "2." *Chivalry and Romance in the English Renaissance.* Cambridge UK:D.S. Brewer, 2003. Print.

Coleman, Julie. *May 2001 The Gardener's Labyrinth.* Special Collections Department, Library, University of Glasgow, Scotland, United Kingdom. <http://special.lib.gla.ac.uk/exhibns/ month/may200 l.html>.

Ellis, Sian. "Parham house and gardens". *British Heritage* 23.2: 26-(8).

"Enjoy the Perfect Day out This Summer." Times [London, England].

Eras of Elegance. <http://www.erasofelegance.com>.

French, Roger. "Pliny the Elder on Science and Technology by John F. Healy." *The History of Science Society* 93.103.

Gascoigne, George. *Gascoigne's Princely Pleasures, with the Masque, Intended to Have Been Presented before Queen Elizabeth, at Kenilworth Castle in 1575*; London: J.H. Burr etc., 1821. Print.

Gerard, J. *The Herbal or General History of Plants: The Complete 1633 Edition as Revised and Enlarged by Thomas Johnson.* New York: Dover Publications, 1975.

Gristwood, Sarah. *Elizabeth & Leicester, Power, Passion, Politics.* New Yark, New York: Vicking, Penguin Group, 2007.

Harvey, John. "An Elizabethan Seed-List". *Garden History* 23.2, Winter, 1995: 242-245.

Henderson, Paula. "Sir Francis Bacon's Water Gardens at Gorhambury." *Garden History Society.* 20.2 1992: 116-131.

Hill, Thomas. *A most briefe andpleasaunte treatise, teachyng how to dresse, sowe, and set a garden (And nowe englished by Thomas Hyll Londiner by Jhon Day for Thomas Hyll).* London: 1558 <http://gateway.proquest.com/openurl?ctx_ver=Z39.88 2003&res_id=xri:eebo&rft_val_fmt=&rft_id=xri:eebo:image: 180798>

Hobhouse, Penelope. *The Story of Gardening.* London: Darling Kindersley Limited, 2002.

Howes, Laura L. *Chaucer's Gardens and the Language of Convention.* Gainesville, FL: University of Florida, 1997. Print.

Ind, Jo. "The Birmingham Post: A garden fit to woo a queen." *The (England) Birmingham Post.* 2009.

Keen, Mary. *The Glory of the English Garden.* London: Bulfinch Press, 1989.

Kenilworth Castle Garden IGardenVisit.com, the Garden Landscape Guide. *Gardenvisit.com the Garden Landscape Guide.* Ed. Tom Turner. Garden History Encyclopedia, 2008. <http://www.gardenvisit.com/garden/kenilworth_castle_garden>.

Langstaff, Margaret. *A Bit of Paradise in the Backyard.* Publishers Weekly 241.6 Feb 1994: 58(5). Academic OneFile. Gale. Washburn Univ-Mabee Library. <http://0find.galegroup.com.topekalibraries.info/itx/start.do?prodId=AONE>.

Marsh, Betsa. *Kenilworth Castle Plants New Elizabethan Garden.* Suite 1ol.com Media Inc. <http://englandtravel.suite101.com/article.cfm/kenilworthcastleplants newelizabethangarden>.

Martyn, Trea. "Busy Lizzie." *History Today* Nov 2008: 58.11-70(2).

Ros, Maggi. "Renaissance Sites and Elizabethan Resources." *Renaissance The Elizabethan World 2009.* <http://elizabethan.org/sites.html>.

Rush, Kim. *The Coronation Procession of Elizabeth I: The Pageants that Created Elizabeth on Her Path to Westminster Abbey. suite1001.com 2009.* <http://tudorhistory.suitelol.com>.

Scott, Walter. *Kenilworth.* New York: Dodd, Mead, 1956. Print.

Sharpe, Henry, Printer. *A Concise History and Description of Kenilworth Castle, from Its Foundation to the Present Time. Google.* Google Books. <http://www.books.google.com/ books?id=efYVAAAA...>.

Stewart, Michael. "Heraldry, Chivalry & Renaissance." *Heraldry, Chivalry & Renaissance Gallery of Medallions.* Quick Silver Mint. 2004. <http://www.quicksilvermint.com/medallions/pages/heraldic-rose.htm>.

Stirling, Brents. "The Philosophy of Spenser's "Garden of Adonis'." *PMLA: Publication of the Modern Language Association of America.* 49.2 1934: 501.

Taylor, Christopher. *Parks and Gardens of Britain: a Landscape History from the Air.* Edinburgh: Edinburgh UP, 1998. Print.

Warwickshire Museum and County Record Office. *Bear and Ragged Staff.* http://www.warwickshire.gov.uk/web/corporate/pages.nsf/Links/2AA8F837EFE001B180 256A38003531A9

Webb, John. *Kenilworth Castle and the History a/Kenilworth.* 2010. <http://hearteng.110mb. com/kenilworth.htm#castle>.

Weir, Alison. *The Life a/Elizabeth I.* New York: Ballantine, 1999. Print.

Woodhouse, Elizabeth. "Spirit of the Elizabethan Garden." *Garden History.* Summer, 1999:27.1

List of Illustrations

Natural Recipes from the Author's Family Legacy

It is time to get back to the basics. I have selected just one natural ingredient from our garden - the lavender (Lavandula angustifolia) to start recipes for this first edition of the Elizabethan Gardener's Handbook. I am sure many more will follow. With the instruction and recipes in this book, you will learn how to create natural products for skin, body and hair that create serenity, vitality and inner wellness. Natural, simple and cost-effective remedies can be the basis for long-term skin, body and hair care. And, please remember that your body is a beautiful and faithful friend as well as a storage facility for your spirit - it must be maintained!!

Harvesting herbs

Dry herbs as soon as they are picked to that their beneficial properties are peaked. Gather herbs in early to mid-morning as later in the day the sun has become too hot.

Lavender

Harvest lavender as soon as the bud is mature and well-formed or after the flower has recently opened. They should be dirt-free. Avoid over-drying herbs. Store in a cool, moisture-free place and away from direct sun-light.

FAMILY RECIPES

Lavender Makeup Remover

This can be used as a heavy makeup remover.

1 tablespoon jojobas base oil

10 drops lavender essential oil

7 tablespoons pure vegetable shortening

Over low heat, in a small saucepan, warm the oil and shortening, remove from heat and allow to cool for 10 minutes, add essential oil and stir slowly with a spoon until mixture thickens. Pour into storage. Use within 12 months. Be sure to apply using a soft cloth or fingers up to 1 teaspoon for the whole face and throat areas. Rinse.

Lavender & Roses Cleanser

This multipurpose natural idea can also be used as a face mask and exfoliant. Just apply to cleansed face and let dry for 20 minutes.

5 drops lavender essential oil

2 drops rose otto

1 tablespoon powdered lavender buds

1 tablespoon powdered rose petals

½ cup finely ground while clay

½ cup ground oatmeal

In a plastic bag place all the ingredients except the oils and fasten with a twist on zip close the top. Shake. Add the oils and shake again. Pour into storage. Use within 6 months. To mix the cleanser for use: Put 2 teaspoons of the mixture into a bowl and add 2 teaspoons of water or milk. Stir to make a paste. Use a soft cloth or fingers and massage in circles for 1 minute. Rinse.

Lavender & Strawberry Cleanser

This multipurpose natural idea can also be used as a tooth cleanser and whitener

1 drop lavender essential oil

4 ripe strawberries, sliced

In a small bowl, mash strawberries with a fork. Press the pulp thru a mesh strainer or squeeze thru cheesecloth and catch the juice in a bowl. Add the oil and stir to blend. Use a cloth or fingers and avoid the eye area and massage with fingers for 1 minute. Rinse with cool water.

Lavender Toner

This multipurpose natural idea can be used for teen girls.

6 drops lavender essential oil

1 tablespoon powdered lavender buds

1 cup witch hazel

Using a half-pint jar, combine the ingredients. Store in a cool and dark place for 2 weeks to steep, shake the container every day. After this process, strain the liquid and pour into another storage container. Use within 6 months. Apply 1 teaspoon to the face or more for a body splash. Avoid eyes!!

Lavender Bath Salts

This natural bath idea softens and soothes and the natural essential oil calms the mind and body. It is best to take this bath before going to bed.

15 drops lavender essential oil

½ cup baking soda

½ cup sea salt

In a plastic bag place all the ingredients except the oil. Use within 6 months. To use turn the bath tap full on and put the mix into the tub. Add the lavender oil when the tub is full and swish the water with your hand. Soak for 20 to 30 minutes.

Lavender Powder

This natural powder idea leaves a sweet, delicate, feminine aroma.

200 drops lavender essential oil

½ cup finely powdered lavender buds

1 cup arrowroot

1 cup white clay

1 cup cornstarch

½ cup powdered rose petals

1 cup finely ground white clay

In a large bowl place all the ingredients except the oils and stir slowly or whirl in a food processor until blended. Then, using a mortar and pestle drop the oil with 6 tablespoons of the powder mix until absorbed. Add this oil mixture to the remaining powder and mix slowly or whirl in a food processor for 15 seconds. Pour into airtight storage container and put in a cool, dark place for 3 days. Use within 1 year.

FOR HAIR

Lavender Basic Conditioner

This organic lavender idea leaves hair soft and silky.

20 drops lavender essential oil

½ cup of one of the following: extra-virgin olive, jojoba, avocado or coconut

Put all the ingredients in a bowl and stir. Apply to dry, clean hair, cover hair with spastic wrap or a shower cap. Wrap with a warm, damp towel. The heat helps the oil penetrate and condition your hair. Leave on hair for 30 minutes minimum. Rinse, then lightly shampoo and follow with conditioner if necessary for your hair.

About Lavender

http://www.kansaslavender.com/lavender.html

"Lavender is one of the most remarkable herbs. Its history is interesting, its uses so many, its fragrance so profound, and its colors so varied."

"In recent years, there has been a resurgence to use herbal/homeopathic remedies and aromatherapy."

"Throughout history lavender rated high on the list of multipurpose herbs. The word lavender means "lito wash". Some literature, as well as discussions with WWII veterans, indicate that Lavender was used as an antiseptic in treating the soldiers wounds. Today lavender is used in soaps for its cleansing properties. Lavender facial cleanser is used to reduce acne."

"Recently, our State of Kansas, adopted a new slogan - "Kansas, as big as you think" .. This slogan can be easily identified with culinary uses of Lavender - Lavender, as big as you think. Lavender is used in combination with several herbs to create a mixture named Herbs de Provence. This mixture can be used on baking of any meat (beef or pork roast, baked chicken), as a salt substitute on vegetables (cauliflower, broccoli), or sprinkled sparingly over fresh salad greens. Lavender can be infused in milk, cream, sugar, honey, etc. The infused products can then be used in any recipe. Lavender can be ground and used alone or mixed with other ground spices in making a wide variety of desserts."

"We planted the Grosso and Provence with the plant rows six feet apart and the plants within the rows are four feet apart. This allows room for the plants to breath during the summer. We also place "large" hay bales around the field to protect the plants from the winter winds. Our grandchildren say the hay and Lavender look like a bowl of frosted shredded wheat."

Growing Lavender

"Lavender is a very hardy, drought tolerant plant. It has two requirements: well drained soil and lots of sun. It needs 8 to 12 hours of sun a day during the growing season."

"Lavender prefers well drained soil - sandy type soil. Soils can be amended with sand or the Lavender can be planted in a mound to accomplish the "well drained" effect. The pH should be in the range of 6.0 to 8.0."

"Lavender does not like "wet feet". Watering or ample rain is needed to get plants established. Young plants need to be watched carefully to ensure adequate moisture. Older more mature plants are more drought tolerant."

"Lavender like lime based soil. Be sure to check you pH. Young plants require more nitrogen (bone meal or blood meal) than mature plants. Nitrogen will increase the length of stems for cut flower use. Never use strong fertilizers or manures."

"Lavender does not like high humidity or cold winter winds. Be sure plants have been spaced far enough apart for then to have good air circulation. This is a must to avoid mold/mildew problems. Protection will be needed from cold winter winds."

"Lavender needs to be pruned either in spring and fall or just in the fall. Spring pruning will promote a later blooming time; however, they will need pruning again in fall. Cut the plant back about one-third, but never cut clear to the dead wood."

Harvesting And Drying

"Lavender is harvested at various stages of maturity. This is governed by the intended use of the flower."

"To use as fresh cut flowers, the stems can be cut at any time. Fresh flowers placed in a vase need to have fresh water daily."

"For drying, cut stems when 3 to 5 florets are open. Combine a hand full of stems, place a rubber band around the stems, then hang upside down to dry. Hang the bundle in a cool, dry, dark place for approximately two weeks"

"To use the buds after drying, shuck or rub the buds off the stems, Remove chaff or dried flower petals and stems from the buds."

CPSIA information can be obtained at www.ICGtesting.com
Printed in the USA
BVIW12n0935100416
443634BV00054B/271